AF591321

Drawn to Tunes

Original Irish Tunes and Drawings

by

Anne-Karoline Distel

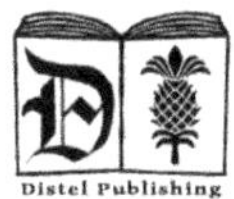

Für Oma

my heritage hero

Foreword

This little album contains drawings of some of my favourite historical sites (mostly) in the South-east of Ireland. It takes you off the beaten track to historically fascinating and/ or magically beautiful places. I have had the privilege of working in two of the oldest buildings in Kilkenny and learning about the people connected with them as well as immersing myself in Irish trad music. This has inspired me to write tunes in honour of Ireland's heritage.

I want to thank all the friends I have made in and through Kilkenny Archaeological Society as well as all my musician and artist friends - you have all made me feel very welcome. Go raibh míle maith agaibh.

For some of the tunes, I give recommendations of others that would make a good set. They can all be found on http://thesession.org.

Furthermore, you can find some tutorials and recordings of the original tunes on my YouTube channel "akathistle music".

Kilkenny, February 2019

Table of Contents

The Secret Garden

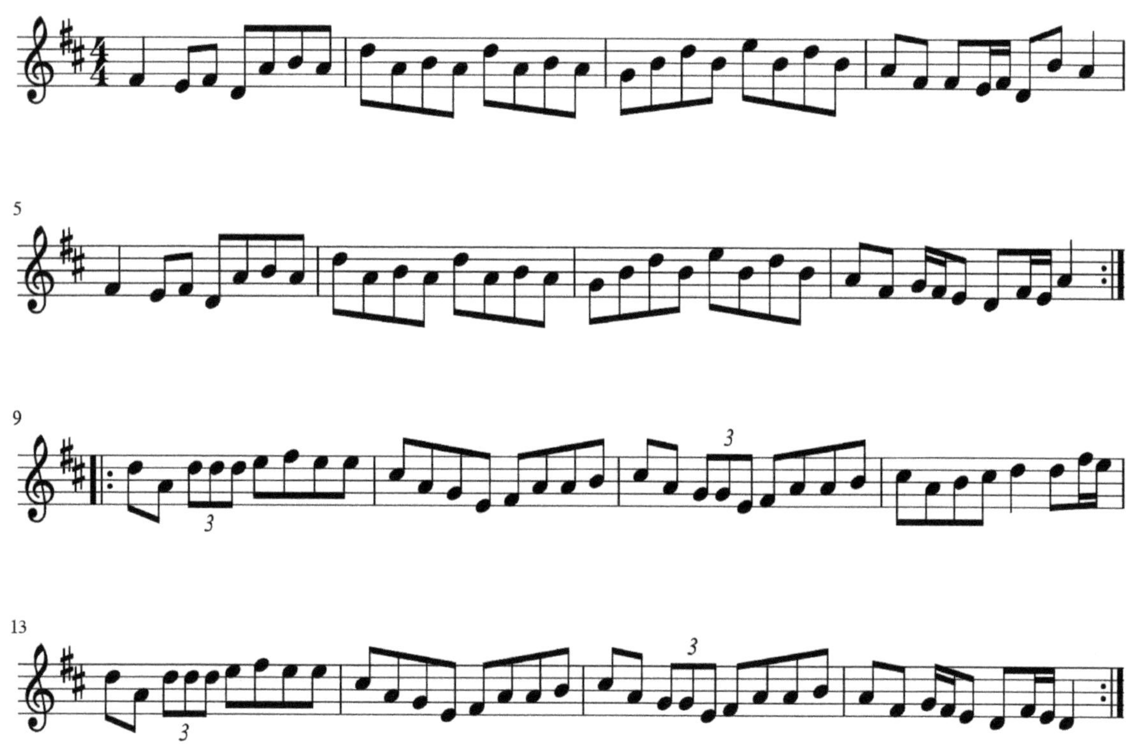

This reel goes well with "The Silver Spear".

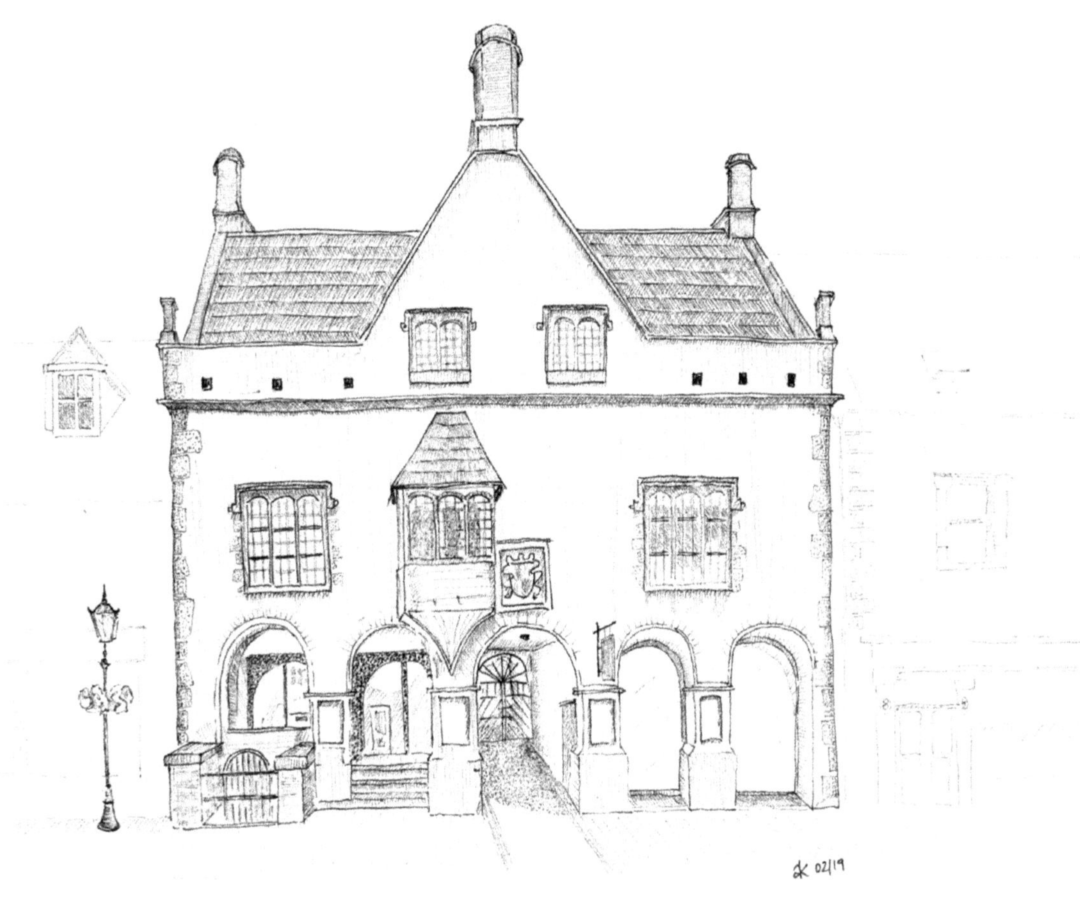

Rothe House, Kilkenny

Hidden from street view, Rothe House features a restored 17th century garden half an acre in size. This unexpected and precious oasis is popular with tourists and locals alike.

The Thrush in the Hawthorne

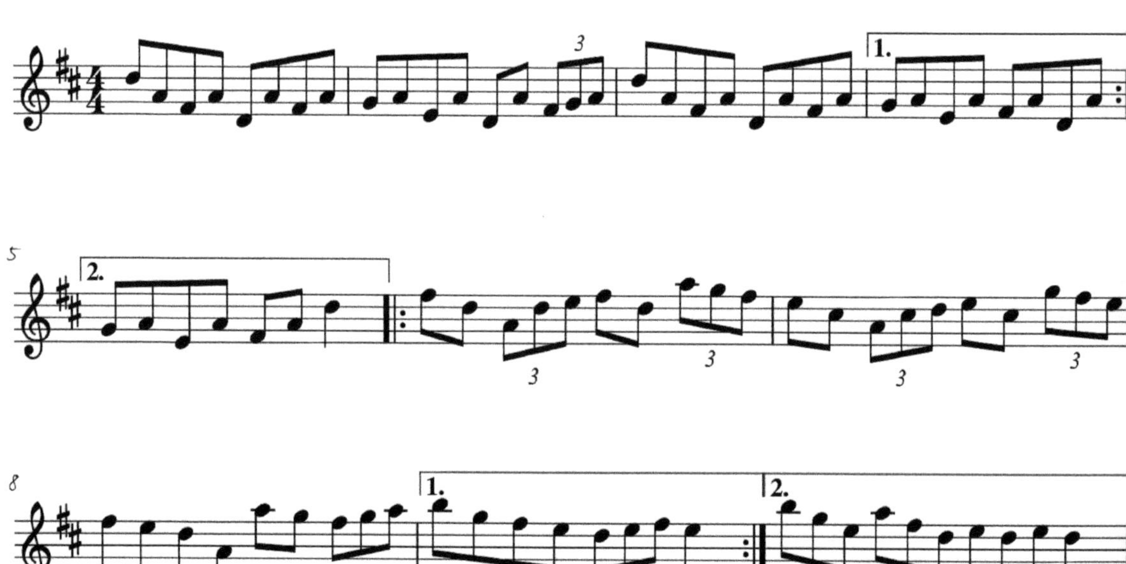

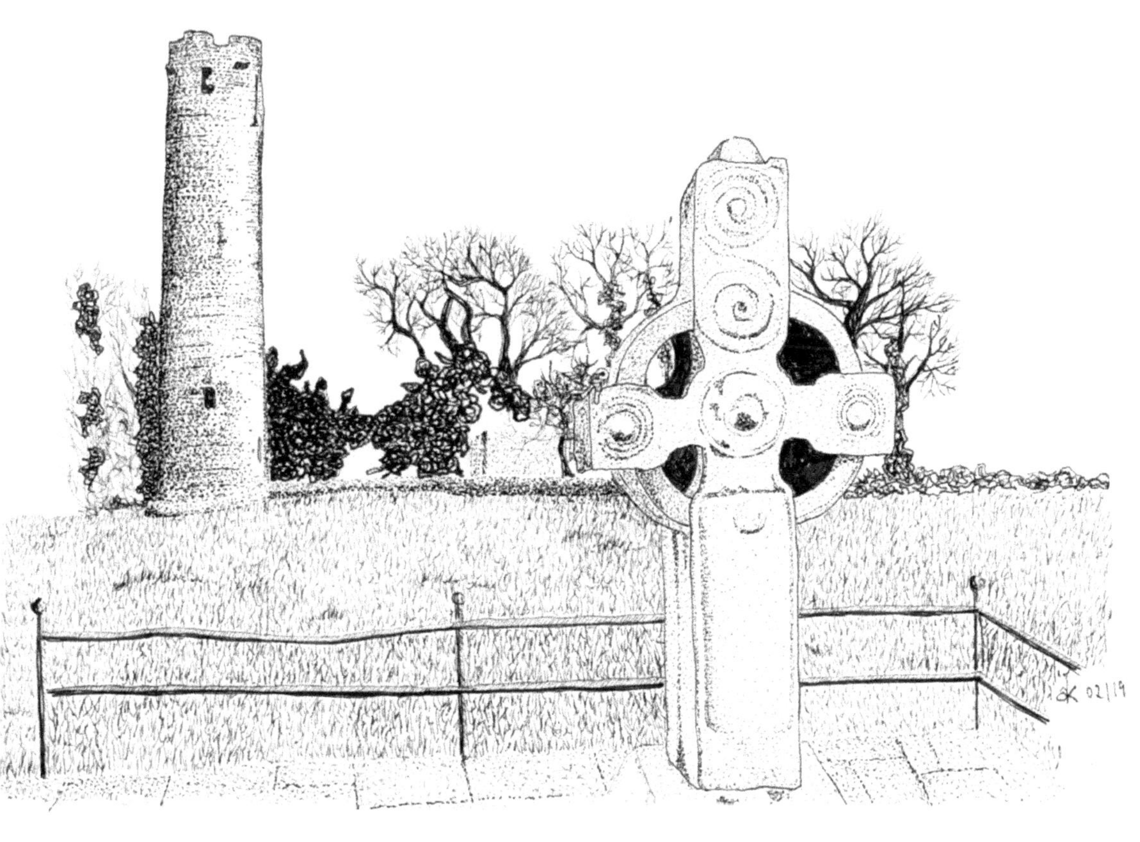

Kilree Monastic Site

Only a short drive from Kells Priory, explorers will discover an old monastic site. At times, the site is guarded by a herd of cows and a bull, so good luck!

The Cooper's Polka

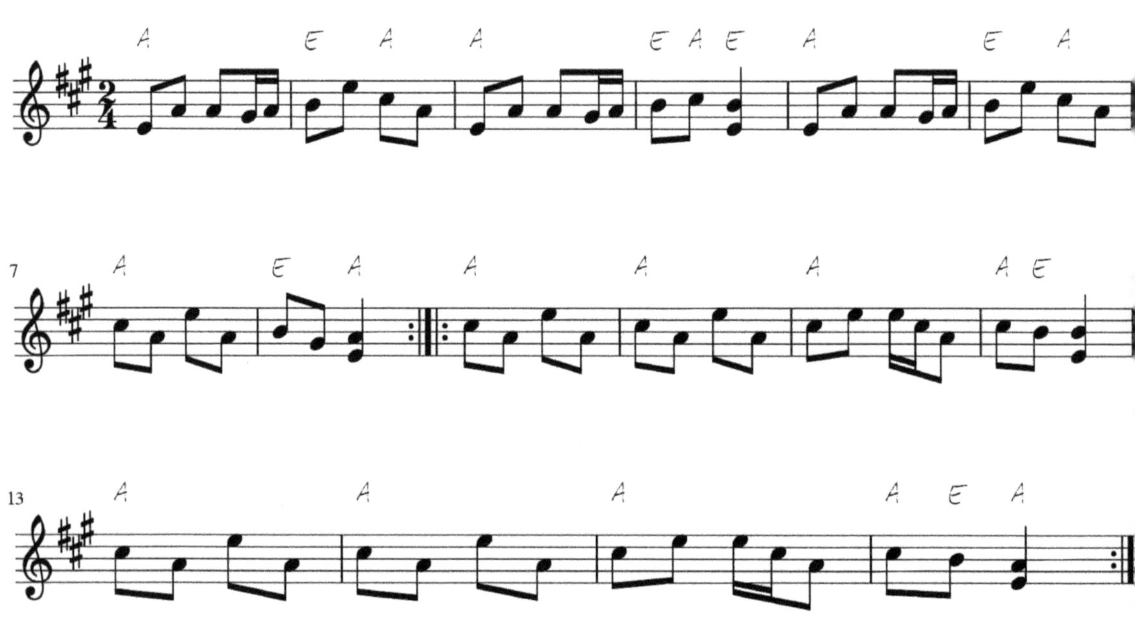

This polka can be followed by "Johnny Kerry's Polka".

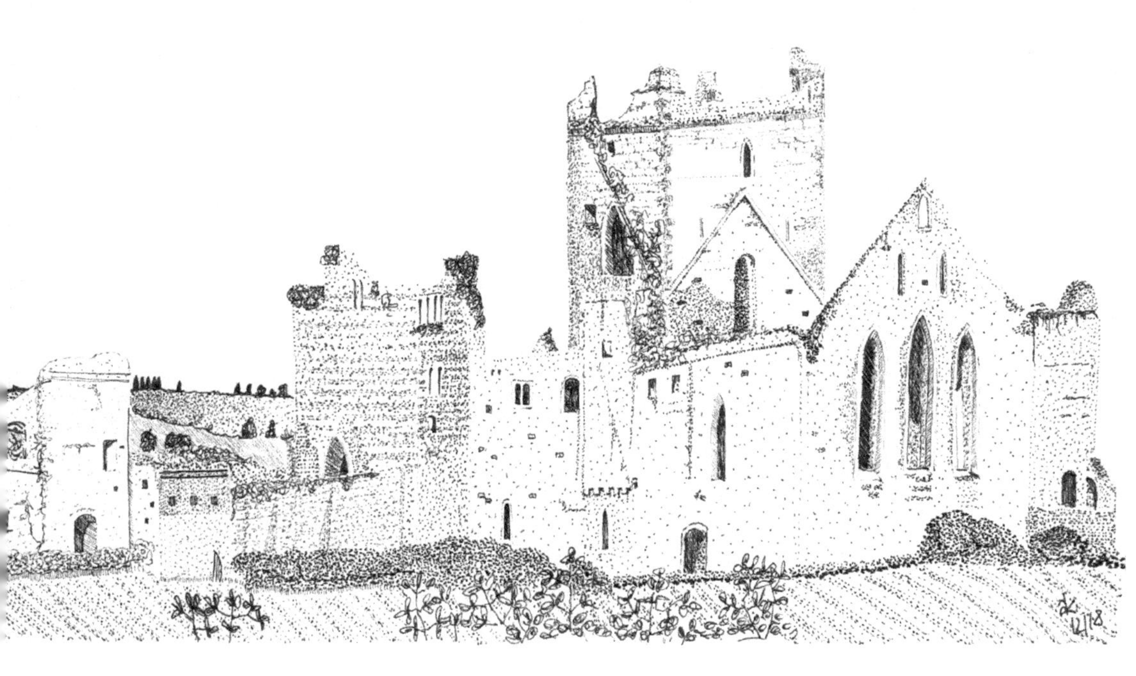

Dunbrody Abbey, Co. Wexford

Dunbrody Abbey is a fine example of Cistercian architecture. It is strategically placed near the confluence of the Campile River and the River Suir. Keys are available in the café across the road.

The Grave in the Grove

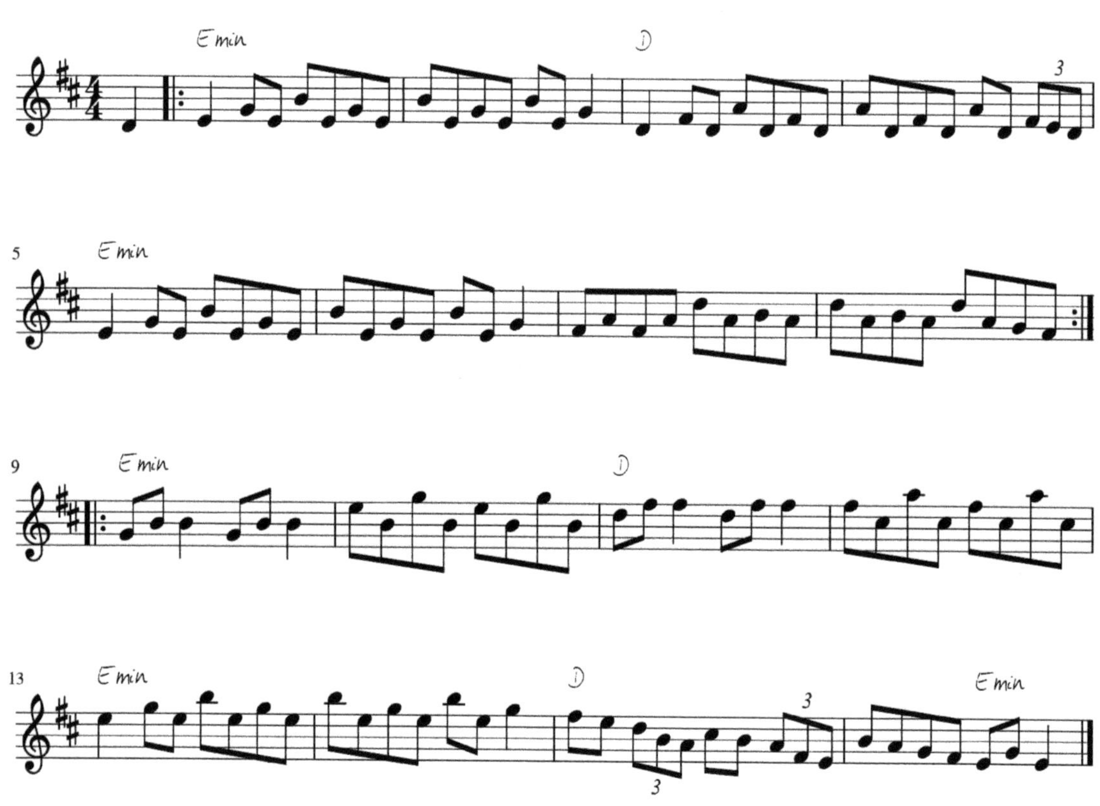

Why not play this reel in a set with "Toss the Feathers"?

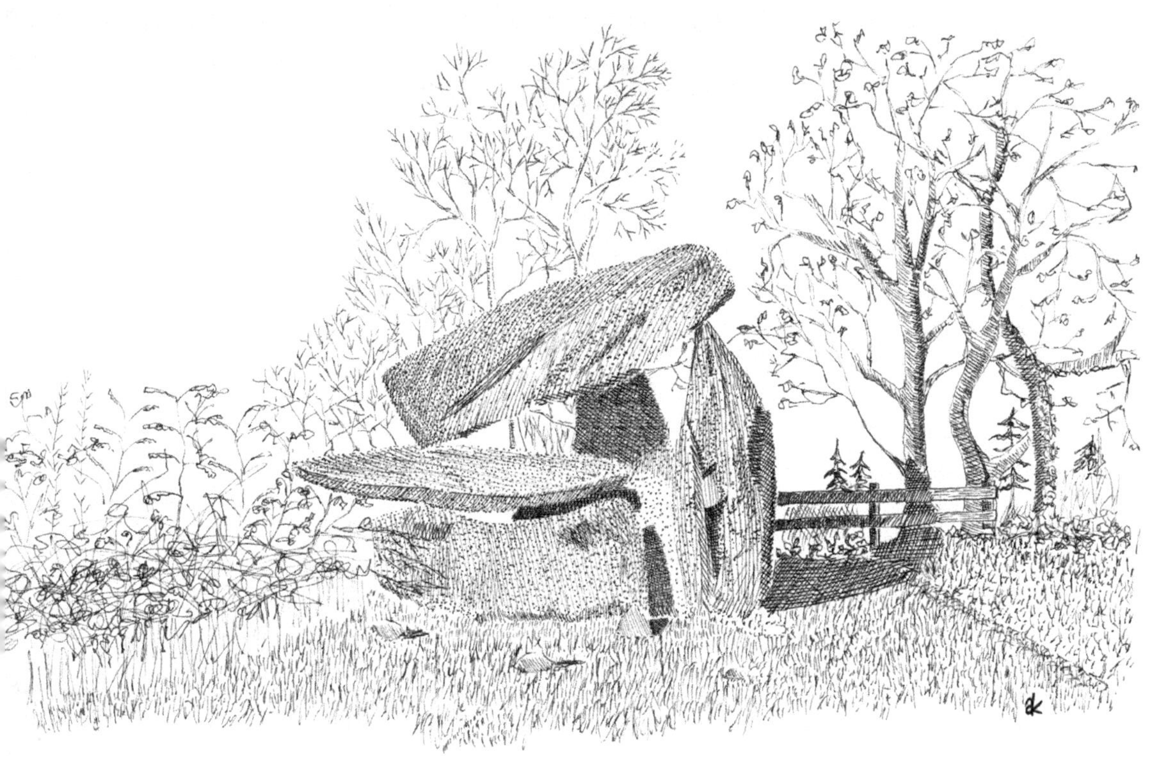

Kilmogue Portal Tomb, Co. Kilkenny

This impressive portal tomb is located in a grove not far from Harristown in South Kilkenny. It is also known as Harristown Dolmen. A bubbling brook provides the background music for this mystical site.

The Mermaid's Dance

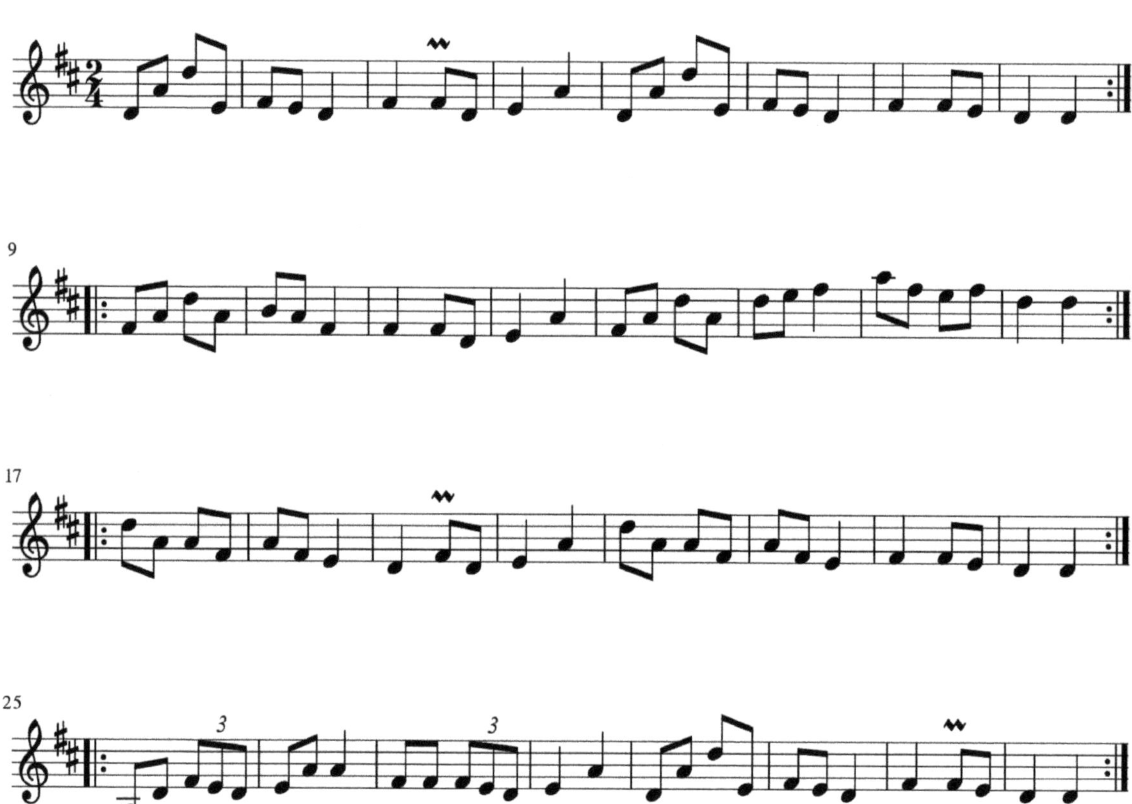

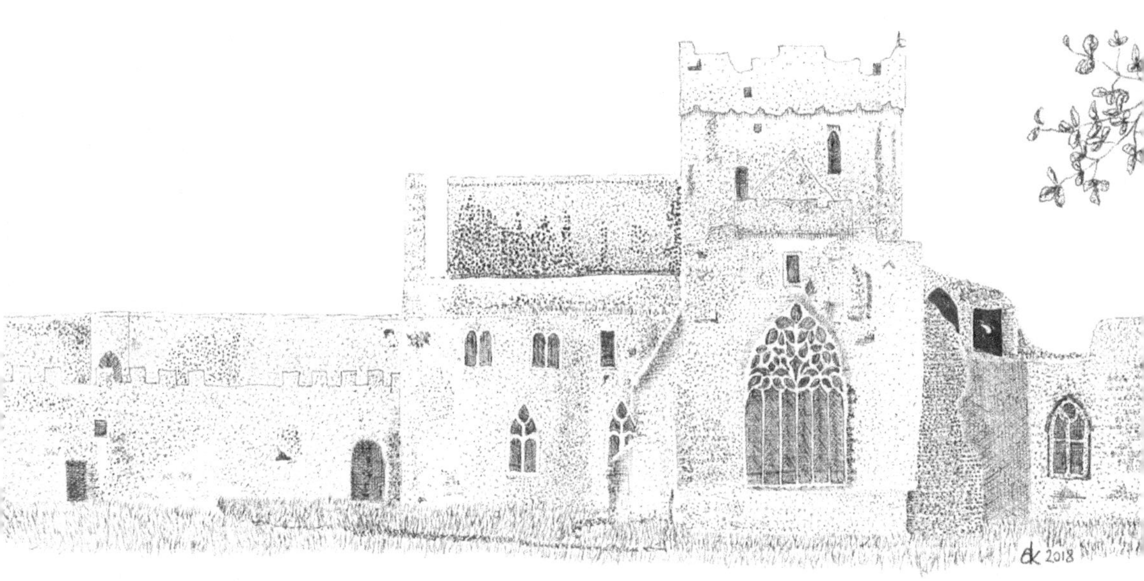

Kilcooley Abbey, Co. Tipperary

This gem with its gorgeously carved window lies hidden in the midst of Kilcooley Woods. The sacristy contains a curious depiction of a mermaid holding a mirror.

Black Tom

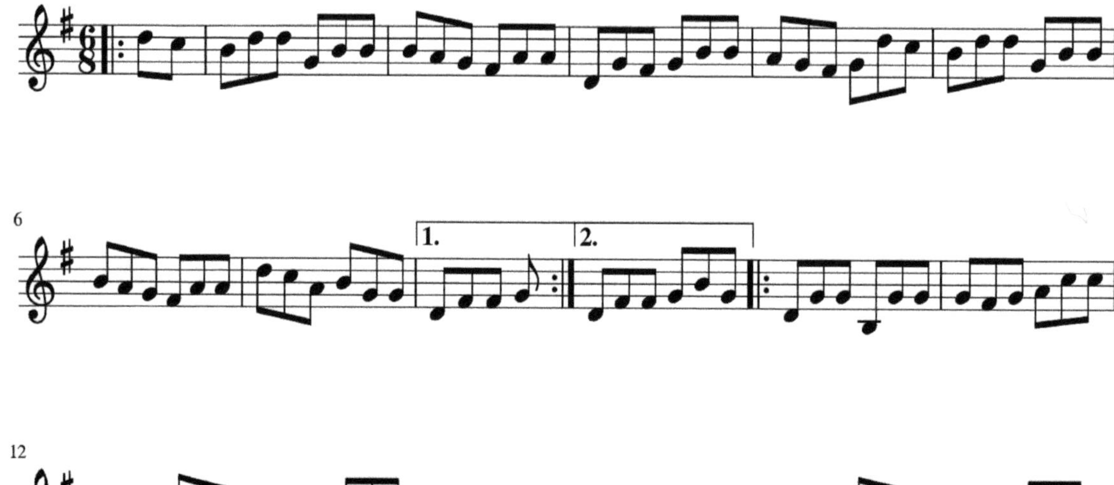

Follow this jig with "The Irish Washerwoman".

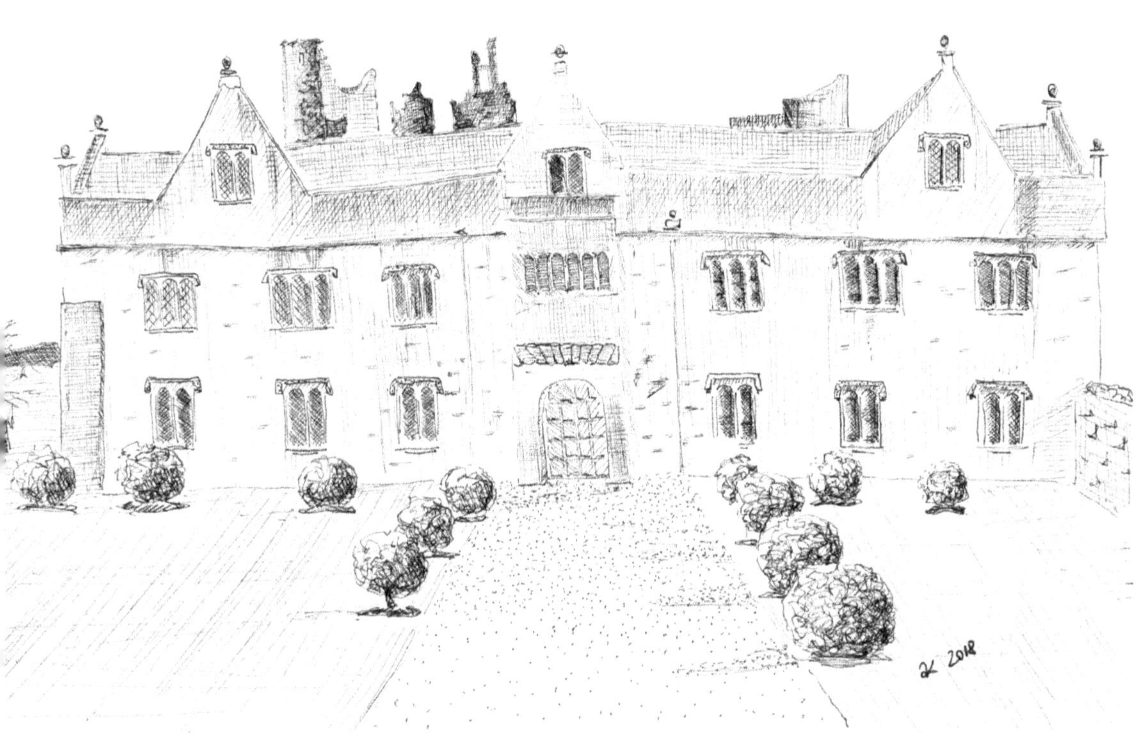

Ormonde Castle, Co. Tipperary

Once home to Thomas Butler, 10th Earl of Ormond, this is another fine example of Tudor architecture and splendour. Thomas (Tomás Dubh = Black Tom) was a cousin of Elizabeth I through her mother Anne Boleyn.

Flying High

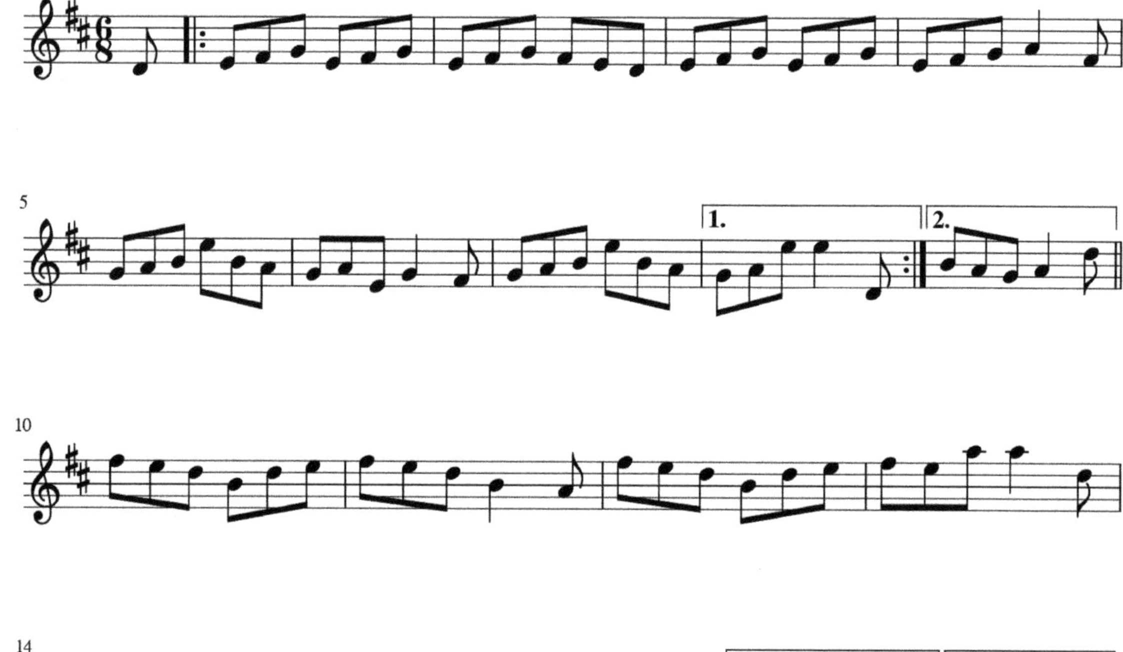

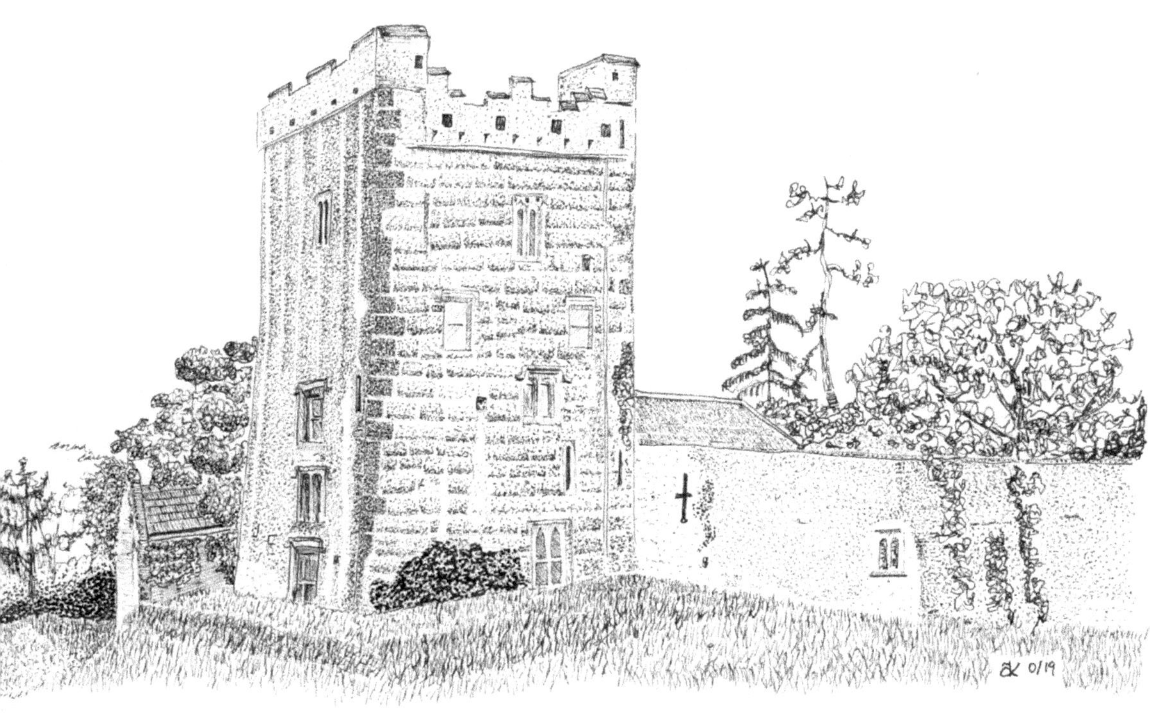

Foulksrath Castle, Co. Kilkenny

This tower house was the launching point (and also very likely landing point) of Kilkenny's first manned flight in 1854. The eccentric Godwin Swifte had built the contraption in his living room.

The Very Auld Triangle

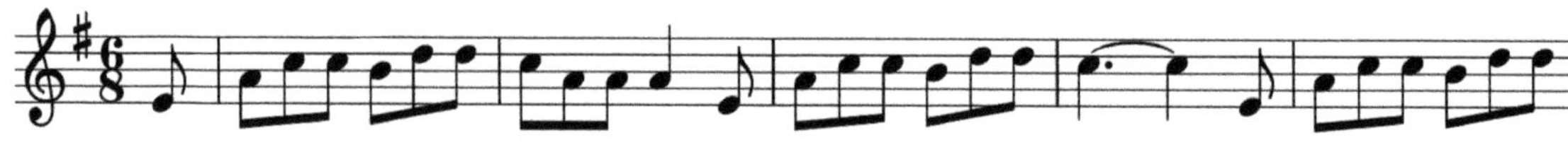

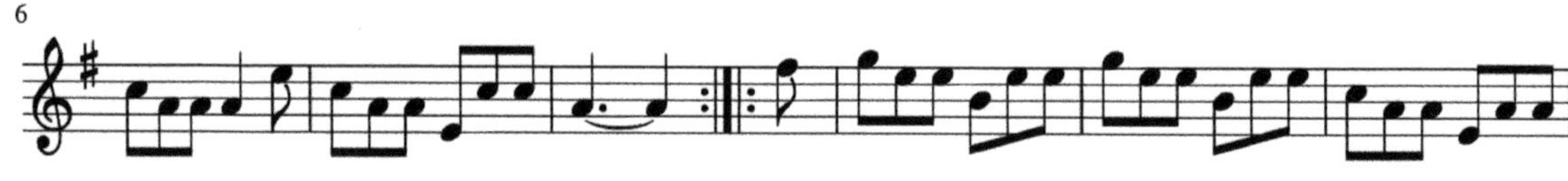

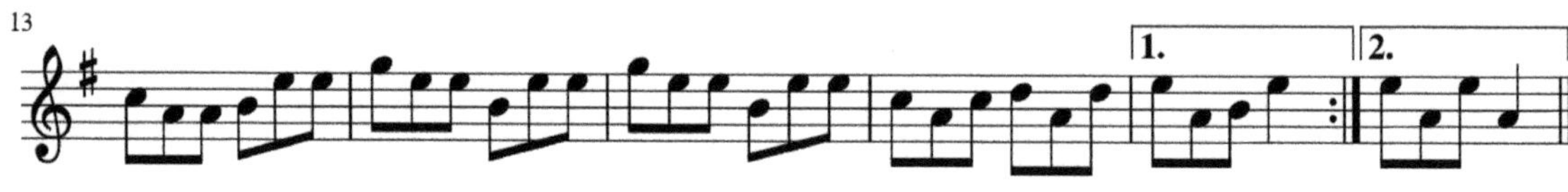

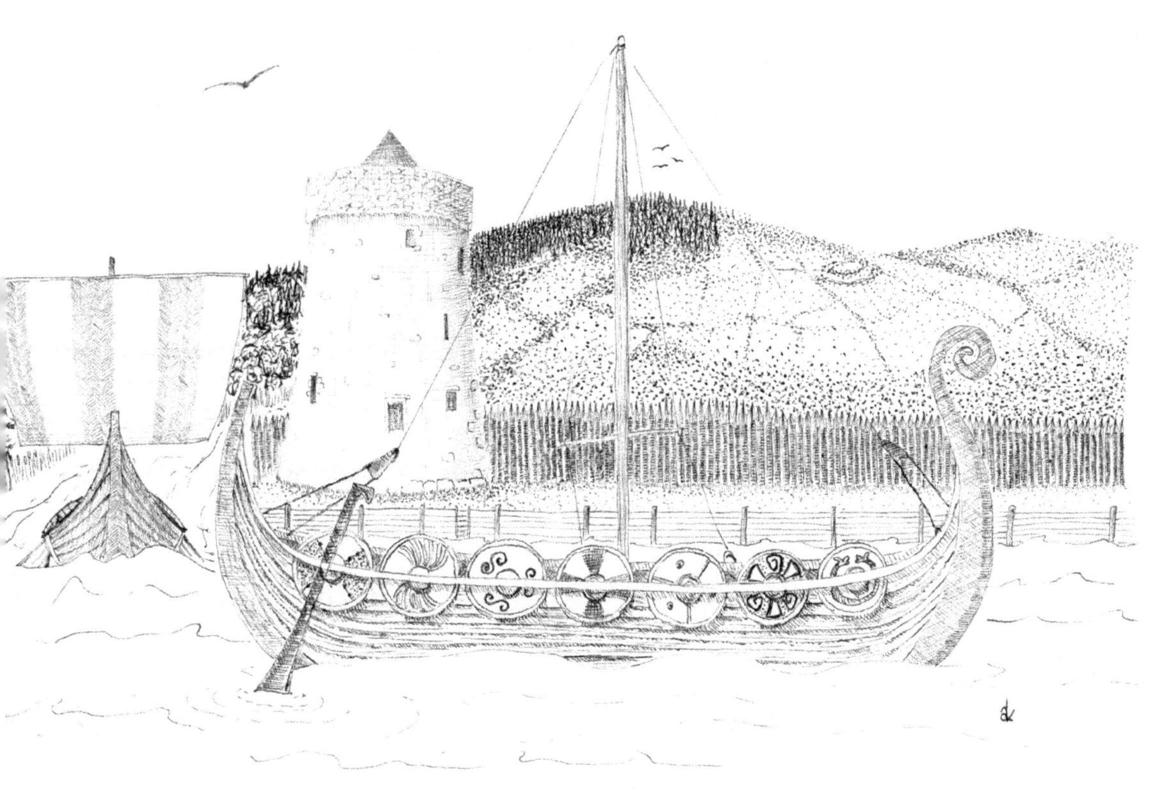

Reginald's Tower, Co. Waterford

This Waterford landmark was built by the Normans on the site of an earlier Viking structure. The museum holds fascinating Viking artefacts like a delicately made kite brooch.

Across the Arches

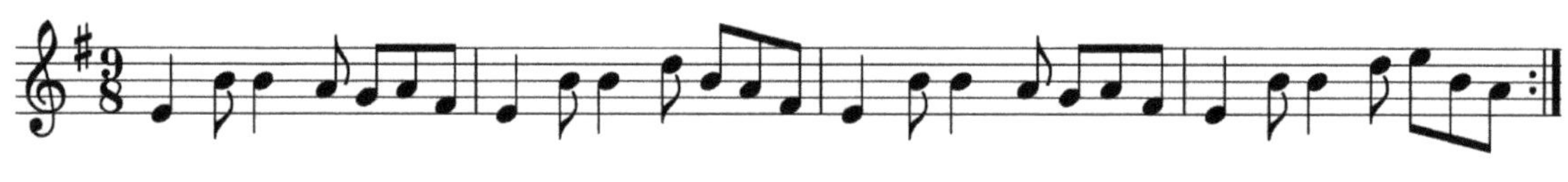

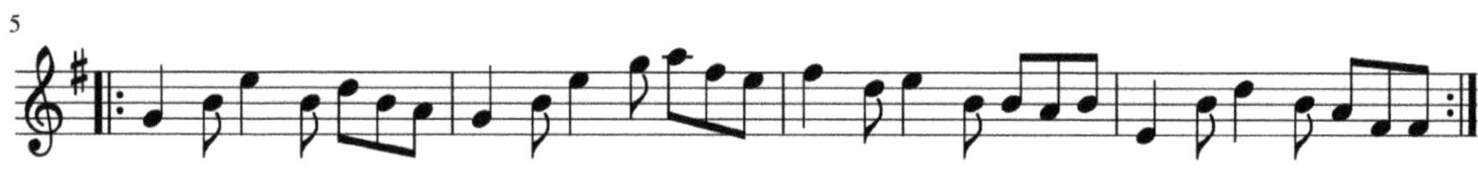

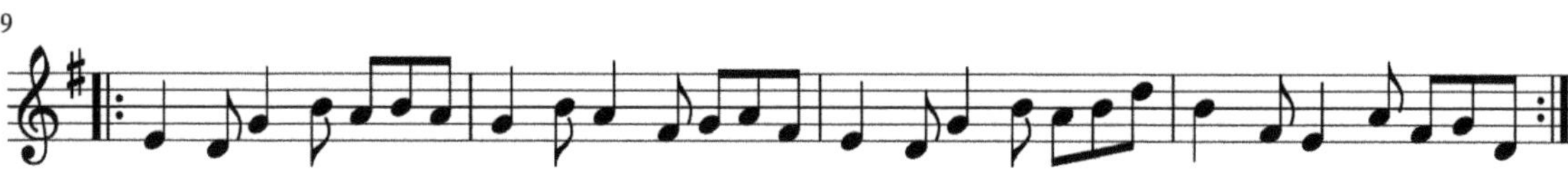

This slip jig might be followed by "The Butterfly" in a set.

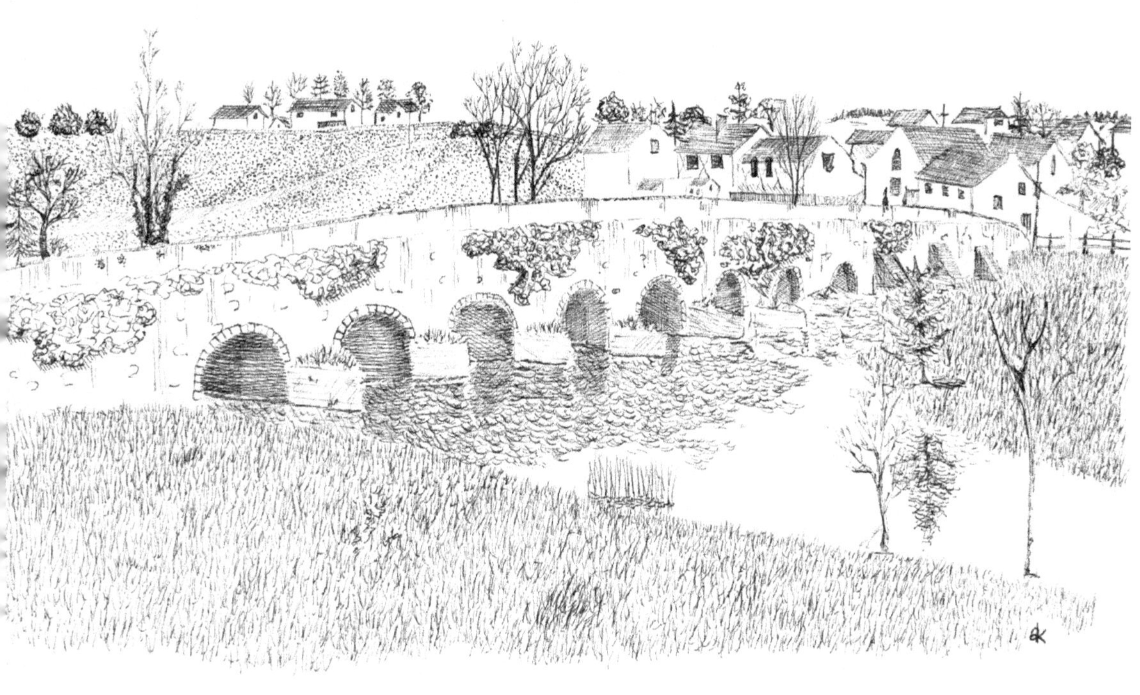

Kells Bridge, Co. Kilkenny

Spanning the King's River, this view shows the older part of the bridge. The other side, facing Mullin's Mills and Kells Priory, was added later to widen the passage across the river.

Sun and Sea

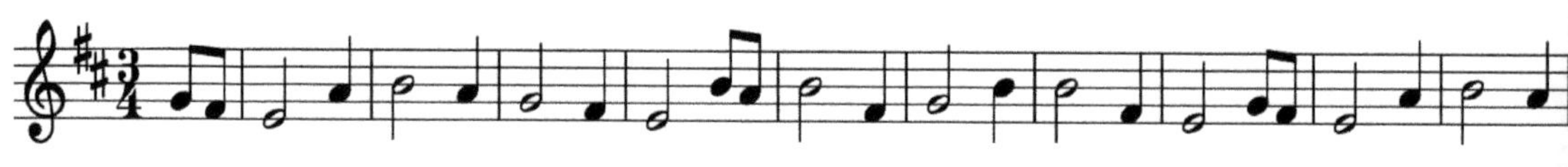

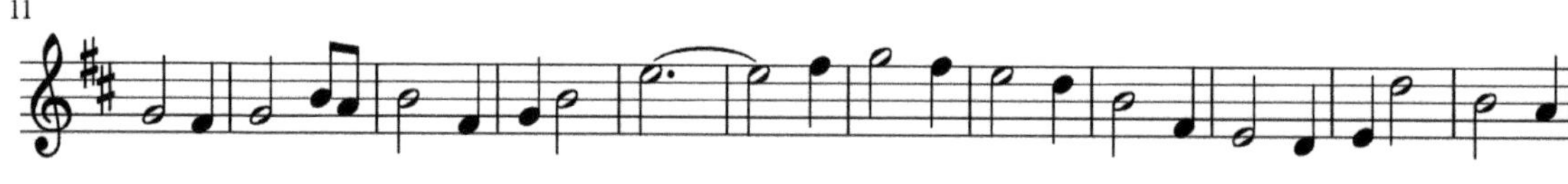

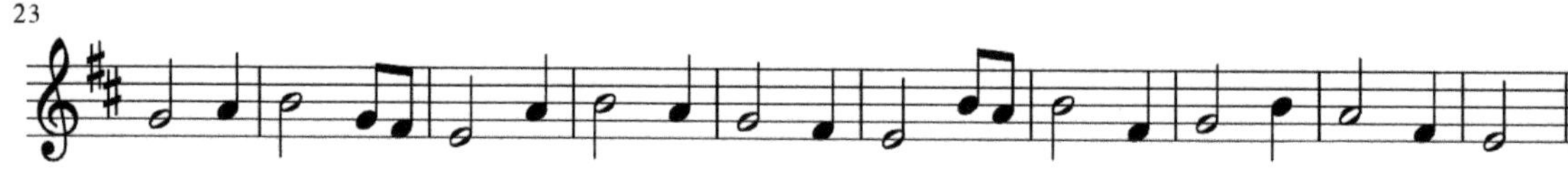

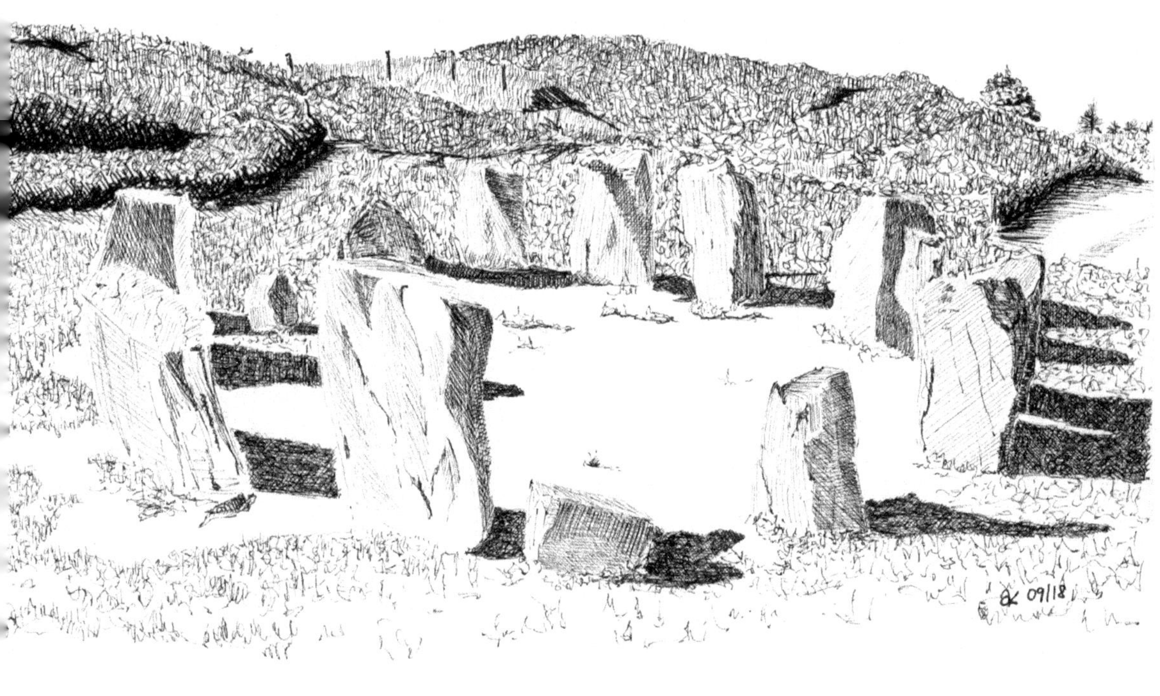

Drombeg Stone Circle, Co. Cork

This magically situated and fascinating ancient place holds special significance for the midwinter solstice. Even today, people gather here to acknowledge and celebrate the morning after the longest night of the year.

The Lonely Monk

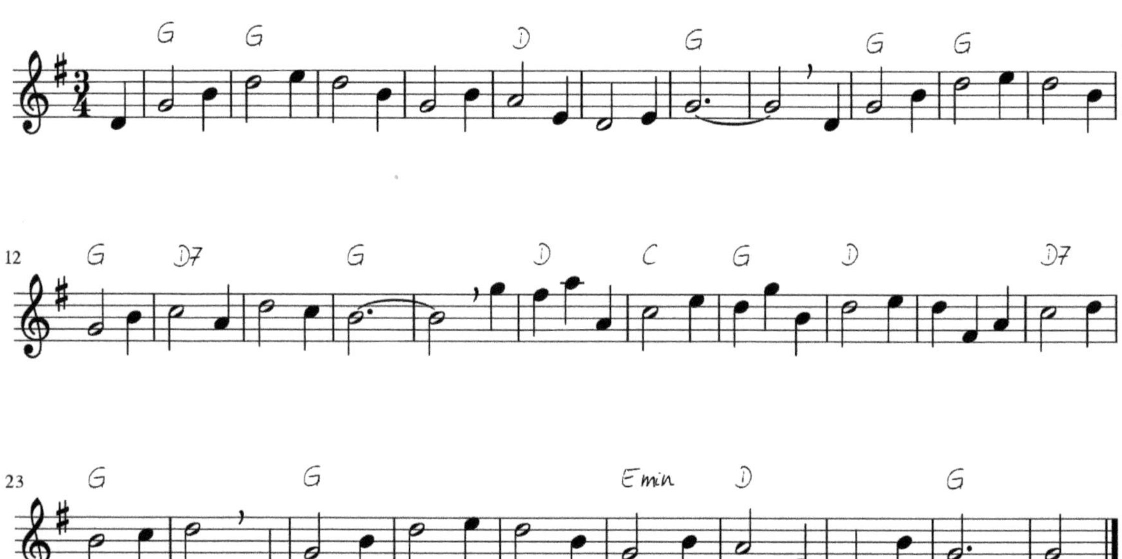

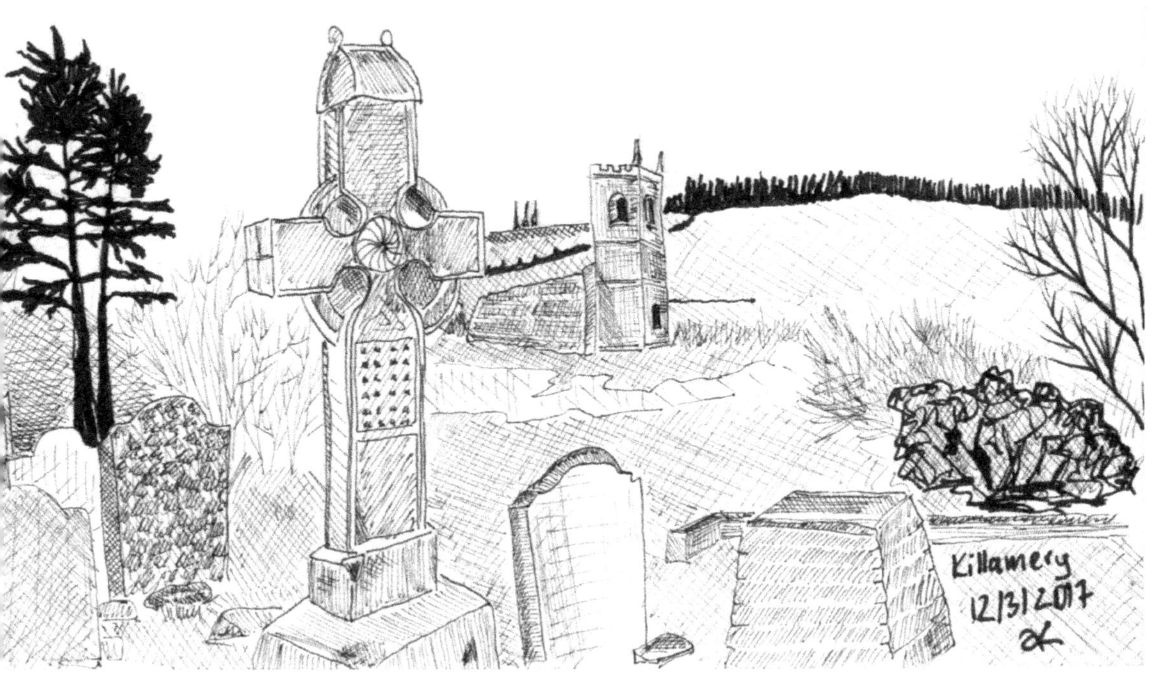

Killamery Monastic Site, Co. Kilkenny

A beautiful silver brooch was discovered at this ancient Christian site, It is now kept in the National Museum. An intricately carved high cross and a church ruin serve as reminders of the once bustling settlement and cultural centre.

Lullaby

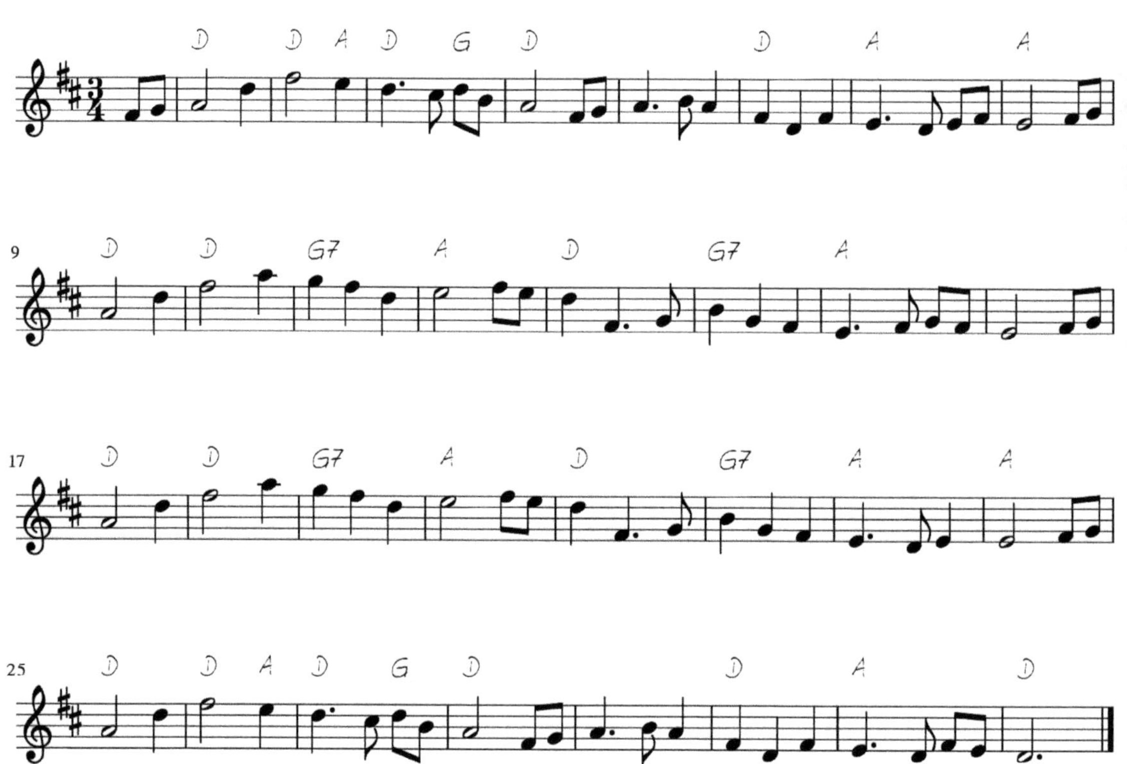

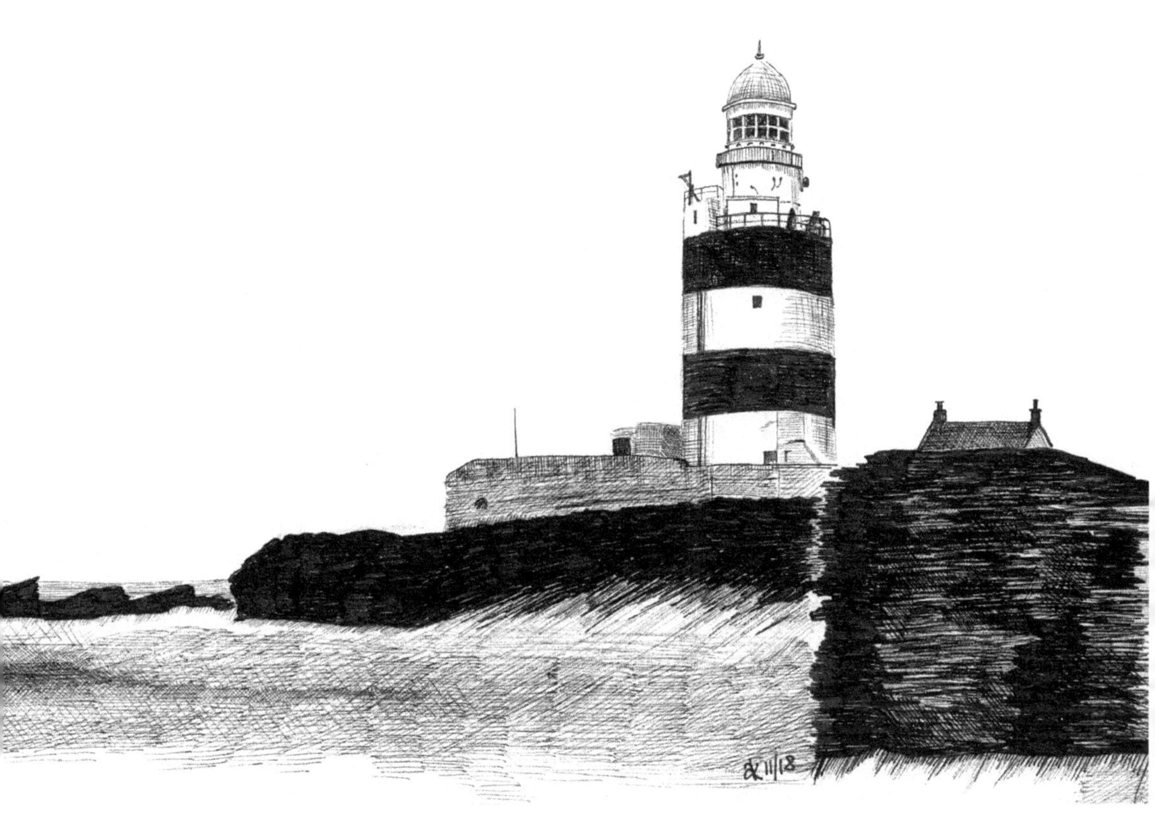

Hook (Head) Lighthouse, Co. Wexford

Hook Lighthouse is one of the oldest lighthouses still operating in the world. It documents the importance of seafaring in this region in times gone by. It is another example of the building boom credited to William Marshall.

Gargoyle's Delight

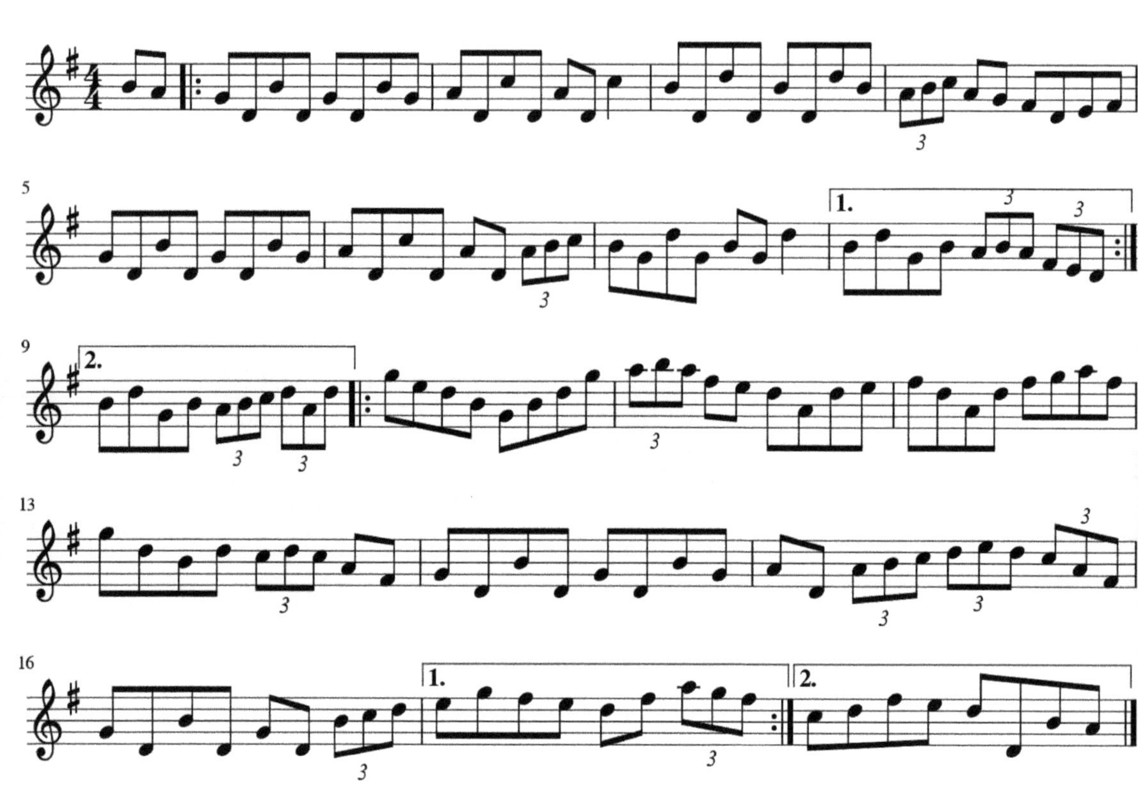

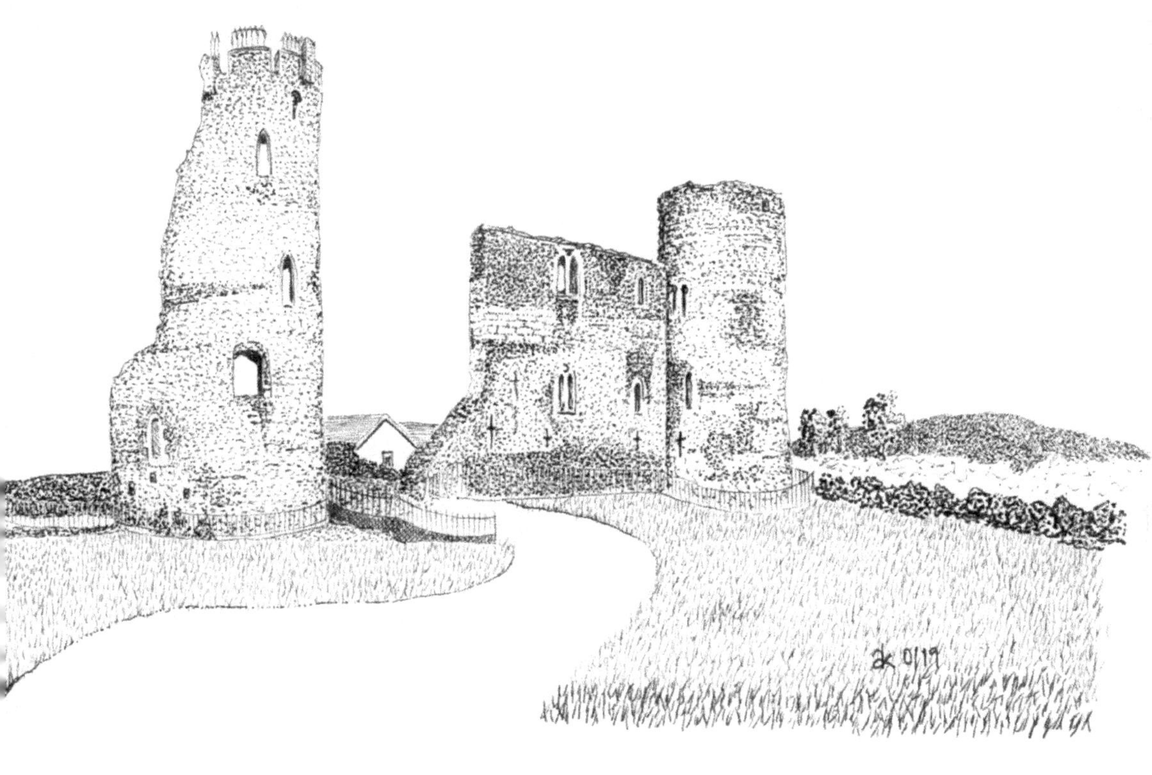

Ferns Castle, Co. Wexford

"The place that launched 1000 ships" - it was Ferns-based Diarmuid Mac Murchadha who invited the first Normans to Ireland for military support. They came to stay, and his daughter Aoife married one of their leaders, Richard 'Strongbow' de Clare in 1170.

ABC Notation of Tunes in Alphabetical Order

T:Across The Nine Arches (slip jig)

C:Anne-Karoline Distel

L:1/8

M:9/8

K:Emin

E2 B B2 A GAF | E2 B B2 d BAF | E2 B B2 A GAF | E2 B B2 d eBA :

: G2 B e2 B dBA | G2 B e2 g afe | f2 d e2 B BAB | E2 B d2 B AFF :

: E2 D G2 B ABA | G2 B A2 F GAF | E2 D G2 B ABd | B2 F E2 A FGD :|

T:Black Tom (jig)

C:Anne-Karoline Distel

L:1/8

M:6/8

K:G

|: dc | Bdd GBB | BAG FAA | DGF GBB | AGF Gdc |

Bdd GBB // BAG FAA | dcA BGG /1 DFF G :/2 DFF GBG

|: DGG B,GG | GFG Acc | cBA BGG | DGF GBG |

DGG B,GG | GFG Acc | ecA BGG | DEF GBG :|

T:Flying High (jig)

C:Anne-Karoline Distel

L:1/8

M:6/8

K:Emin

D /: EFG EFG | EFG FED | EFG EFG | EFG A2 F |

GAB eBA | GAE G2 F | GAB eBA /1 GAe e2 D :/2 BAG A2 d ||

fed Bde | fed B2 A | fed Bde | fea a2 d |

edB edB | dBA dBA | GAE DGA /1 BAG A2 d :/2 BGD E2 ||

T:Gargoyle's Delight (hornpipe)

C:Anne-Karoline Distel

L:1/8

M:4/4

K:G

BA |: GDBD GDBG | ADcD AD c2 | BDdD BDdB | (3ABc AG FDEF |

DBD GDBG | ADcD AD (3ABc | BGdG BG d2 || BdGB (3ABA (3FED :|

2 BdGB (3ABc (3dAd ||: gedB GBdg | (3aba fe dAde | fdAd fgaf |

gdBd (3cdc AF | GDBD GDBG | AD (3ABc (3ded (3cAF |

GDBD GD (3Bcd || egfe df (3agf :|2 cdfe dDBA ||

```
T:Lullaby
C:Anne-Karoline Distel
L:1/8
M:3/4
K:D
FG | A4 d2 | f4 e2 | d3 c dB | A4 FG | A3 B A2 | F2 D2 F2 | E3 D EF |
E4 FG | A4 d2 | f4 a2 | g2 f2 d2 | e4 fe | d2 F3 G | B2 G2 F2 |
E3 F GF | E4 FG | A4 d2 | f4 a2 | g2 f2 d2 | e4 fe | d2 F3 G |
B2 G2 F2 | E3 D E2 | E4 FG | A4 d2 | f4 e2 | d3 c dB |
A4 FG | A3 B A2 | F2 D2 F2 | E3 D FE | D6 ||
```

```
T:Sun and Sea
C:Anne-Karoline Distel
L:1/4
M:3/4
K:Emin
G/F/ | E2 A | B2 A | G2 F | E2 B/A/ | B2 F | G2 B | B2 F | E2 G/F/ |
E2 A | B2 A | G2 F | G2 B/A/ | B2 F | G B2 | e3- | e2 f | g2 f | e2 d |
B2 F | E2 D | E d2 | B2 A | G2 A | B2 G/F/ | E2 A | B2 A | G2 F /E2
B/A/ | B2 F | G2 B | A2 F | E2 ||
```

T:The Cooper's Polka

C:Anne-Karoline Distel

L:1/8

M:2/4

K:A

EA AG/A/ | Be cA | EA AG/A/ | Bc /EB/2 |

EA AG/A/ | Be cA | cA eA | BG /EA/2 :|

|: cA eA | cA eA | ce e/c/A | cB /EB/2 |

cA eA | cA eA | ce e/c/A | cB /EA/2 :|

T:The Grave in the Grove

C:Anne-Karoline Distel

L:1/8

M:4/4

K:Emin

D2 |: E2 GE BEGE | BEGE BE G2 | D2 FD ADFD | ADFD AD (3FED |

E2 GE BEGE | BEGE BE G2 | FAFA dABA | dABA dAGF :|

|: GB B2 GB B2 | eBgB eBgB | df f2 df f2 | fcac fcac

e2 ge bege | bege be g2 | fe (3dBA cB (3AFE | BAGF EG E2 :||

T:The Lonely Monk (waltz)

C:Anne-Karoline Distel

L:1/4

M:3/4

K:G

D | G2 B | d2 e | d2 B | G2 B | A2 E | D2 E | G3- | G2 D |

G2 B | d2 e | d2 B | G2 B | c2 A | d2 c | B3- | B2 g |

f a A | c2 e | d g B | d2 e | d F A | c2 d | B2 c |

d2 D | G2 B | d2 e | d2 B | G2 B | A2 E | D2 B | G3- | G2 ||

T:The Mermaid's Dance (polka)

C:Anne-Karoline Distel

L:1/8

M:2/4

K:D

DA dE | FE D2 | F2 PFD | E2 A2 | DA dE | FE D2 | F2 FE | D2 D2 :|

|: FA dA | BA F2 | F2 FD | E2 A2 | FA dA | de f2 | af ef | d2 d2 :|

|: dA AF | AF E2 | D2 PFD | E2 A2 | dA AF | AF E2 | F2 FE | D2 D2 :|

|: A,D (3FED | EA A2 | FF (3FED | E2 A2 | DA dE | FE D2 | F2 PFE | D2

D2 :||

```
T:The Secret Garden (reel)
C:Anne-Karoline Distel
L:1/8
M:4/4
K:D
F2 EF DABA | dABA dABA | GBdB eBdB | AF FE/F/ DB A2 |
F2 EF DABA | dABA dABA | GBdB eBdB | AF G/F/E DF/E/ A2 ::
dA (3ddd efee | cAGE FAAB | cA (3GGE FAAB | cABc d2 df/e/ |
dA (3ddd efee | cAGE FAAB | cA (3GGE FAAB | AF G/F/E DF/E/ D2 :|
```

```
T:The Thrush in the Hawthorne (reel)
C:Anne-Karoline Distel
L:1/8
M:4/4
K:D
dAFA DAFA | GAEA DA (3FGA | dAFA DAFA |1 GAEA FADA :|2 GAEA FA d2
|: fd (3Ade fd (3agf | ec (3Acd ec (3gfe |
fedA ag (3fga || bgfe (3def e2 :|2 (3bge (3afd (3ede d2 ||
```

T:The Very Auld Triangle (jig)

C:Anne-Karoline Distel

L:1/8

M:6/8

K:G

E | Acc Bdd | cAA A2 E | Acc Bdd | c3- c2 E | Acc Bdd |

cAA A2 e | cAA Ecc | A3- A2 :: f | gee Bee | gee Bee | cAA EAA |

cAA Bee | gee Bee | gee Bee | cAc dAd || eAB e2 :|2 eAe A2 ||

www.ingramcontent.com/pod-product-compliance
Ingram Content Group UK Ltd.
Pitfield, Milton Keynes, MK11 3LW, UK
UKHW051126260726
13967UKWH00010B/2884